THE AWAKENING

A COLLECTION OF POEMS

THE AWAKENING

A COLLECTION OF POEMS

By Stuart Peacock

APEX PUBLISHING LTD

First published in 2016 by
Apex Publishing Ltd
12A St. John's Road, Clacton on Sea, Essex, CO15 4BP, United Kingdom

www.apexpublishing.co.uk

Copyright © 2016 by Stuart Peacock
The author has asserted his moral rights

British Library Cataloguing-in-Publication Data
A catalogue record for this book
is available from the British Library

ISBN: 978-1-911476-33-7

All rights reserved. This book is sold subject to the condition that no part of this book is to be reproduced in any shape or form. Or by way of trade, stored in a retrieval system or transmitted in any form or by any means, electronic, mechanical, photocopying, recording, be lent, re-sold, hired out or otherwise circulated in any form of binding or cover other than that in which it is published and without a similar condition, including this condition being imposed on the subsequent purchaser, without prior permission of the copyright holder.

Typeset in 12pt Palatino Linotype

Editor: Kim Kimber
Production Manager: Chris Cowlin
Cover Designer: Hannah Blamires

Publisher's Note:
The views and opinions expressed in this publication are those of the authors and are not necessarily those of Apex Publishing Ltd

CONTENTS

THE AWAKENING	1
AQUARIUS	3
THE DREAM ROOM	5
MIND OF MURDER	7
CHASING YOUR TURNING HEAD	9
BEAUTY FROM BLACKNESS	11
CRYSTAL EYES	12
THE SILENT FORCE	14
DREAM'S END	15
REVOLUTION'S DUST	16
THE LAST TRAIN	18
SEED OF DOUBT	19
UNQUENCHABLE	21
THE STARDUST SHADOW	23
THE SECRET LIBRARY	25
THE CONTROLLER	27
STOLEN HEARTS	30
GUARDIAN OF GOLD	32
SHALLOW AS TIME	33
THE ETERNAL DEEP	35
THE SIMPLE JOY	36
THE RAIN OF REDEMPTION	38
THE VICIOUS VEIL	39
AN ODE TO ORANGE	41
TIDE OF TIME	44
THE GENTLE DRAGON	46
THE SURFACING	47
ABOUT THE AUTHOR	49

www.apexpublishing.co.uk

THE AWAKENING

It's an elusive creature, that creative spark.
Flashing fragments and moments melted away
In the invasive heat of reality, lost to the dark,
After the cycle of the same old steps, ends the day.

Long may it slumber if we do not stop to ponder
The potential all around us, be it rushing or lifeless.
If we detour from day-to-day, to stare in wonder
We realise the creativity the world can possess.

***

Look at those eyes, pools of personality and stories,
And lonely castles lying dormant after past glories.
Choked by twisting branches and jet-black thorns,
Their tendrils slowly sucking life out of our lawns.

Observe ruined buildings with mouths agape,
And sticks clamped together into a star-shape.
Near-fading footprints stamped into mud,
Close-to-dying leaves drenched in blood.

Our ears ring with noise confined to thought,
A symphony of recollection, sounds we caught.
Silent songs heard from a stationary violin,
The echoing words of virtue, as well as sin.

Look at the others who have chosen this deviation,
They have lost much, bore the same frustration.
But on this new route, the essence is recovering,
The inner creature absorbs all, the body unmoving.

Hollow-eyed masks filled with deeper meaning,
Half-open, half-closed, a state of dreaming.
Masks with faces that don't want to be found,
Mouths wide open but yet they emit no sound.

***

It's an elusive creature, that creative spark.
Mending broken pieces, showing us the way,
A torch that guides us through the dark,
But its power charged by the light of day.

AQUARIUS

I stride across the pallid terrain, towards
A huge, gaping void, stretched and wide.
Barefoot I go, sand stubbornly sticking
Like ashes of the past between my toes.

The sky above becomes a brash auburn,
Purple streaks painted on in patches,
Clouds congealing like candyfloss,
Like a childish game, eyes fix upon them,
Until they become something else.

I am alone, surrounded only by
Two great rifts that wrap the world.
Here, they become one, stretching
And vanishing, separating worlds,
Yet connecting them too.

I step into the crystal sea in front of me,
So clear and soothing to the touch.
The grainy remains gone now, I dive in,
Ravaged by cold that becomes euphoria,
Slowly, I become one with the water.

Ecstasy overcomes me, crashing like a wave,
Over withdrawing shore, the past forgotten,
Washing away what is worthless or futile.
The undertow grasps me in, pulling me down
To the fantastic ultramarine under the sky.

I emerge with a splash, foam spraying away,
I am naked, sprawled out like a starfish.
The world goes by still, washing over me,
But still watching over me too.

THE DREAM ROOM

I continue on this vague, static journey,
Through distractions and locked doors.
Blurred apparitions block all ahead of me,
Regrets and remorse infect like ugly sores.

I have no clue who to look for, all I know
Is they are in this labyrinth, somewhere.
I search for the substance of this shadow,
Climbing countless stairs, above a cellar of despair.

Until I find it, I shall roam the halls tirelessly,
Chasing all of those whispers and murmurs
To lift myself from the abyss of jealously,
As there is no solace in envying the others.

But suddenly my solitary vigil is brightened,
When in the hopeless hall, a light is shifting,
To reveal a door unknown, but different.
Could it be my contentment, my lifting?

My shaking hand grips the eagle's wing,
An abstract handle melded onto a mural
Of pearls and emeralds, ever glistening.
In my quest I have seen nothing so beautiful.

As the door flies open, the room I see
Is of four walls, but it knows no bounds
I see no vanishing point, ahead or above me
No ceiling or floor confine these mystic grounds.

Stepping forward, I step back at the same time,
Every surface is glass, a myriad of mirrors.
I breathe heavily, I have returned to the prime,
My mind unlocked, discarding past errors.

The room that contains nothing, but everything,
Projecting millions of images but still only one.
The hallowed centre, the core of our being,
From deep below I return to the light of the sun.

MIND OF MURDER

His axe sits silently by the wall
With its sharp edge, warning us
Of its naked wrath, its raging power
To finish life in a scarlet flourish,
The signature of the remorseless.
He now stands back from it
In quaking, twitching fear.

He stands back, yet nobody is there
No one to wield this terrible tool.
He only sees himself, coldly imprinted
In its steel reflection, always staring,
A face once alight with arrogance,
Now fading, doused of hateful fire,
A broken man, nothing.

The wallpaper is yellowing, crumbling,
Peeling, crackling, and consuming
His very mind, closing in around him.
Its bumpy pattern firmly in his head,
Like the mad wench in the morbid story
He read, those books his only friends
In the world he gave up on.

It's all he can do to fill his time,
He can't move from here, or now,
Entwined in this thick rope of terror
Which the axe cannot cut him from.
It did his bidding some hours ago,
That unspeakable act, stealing
The most valuable thing of all.

The claret splatter is all that remains of her,
The vanquisher's wine, a brutal brushstroke.
But she is still there, accusing, tormenting him.
It's wearing her scarlet dress, and dripping,
Into nothing, the vortex of the icy carpet.
Each and every drip pulsates in his head,
Forever more, with no respite.

Drip, drip, drip.
You, killed, me.
Drip, drip, drip.
You, killed, me.
It matters not how much he says sorry.

CHASING YOUR TURNING HEAD

Chasing your turning head,
Round and round it goes,
I forget your face as it fades,
One I never truly knew at all.

You'd stop and pause for some,
But scarcely would it be me.
I never got to the same track,
But my aching heart kept trying.

You whistled that same old tune,
Merely tolerating my own tempo,
Unwilling to adjust for another
Or give up a second of your runtime.

I ambled through this skipping record,
My feet staying on for the next song,
But your feet had already stepped off,
Hadn't they?

The ride was over for you.
Our song had become strained,
But you kept up our forced dance,
Before letting the needle
Pierce my feelings.

Our rhythm now at an abrupt end.
Too late, I realise the wrong notes.

When I asked what was wrong,
And you said it didn't matter.

When you promised a morning call,
But I awoke to nothing.

When I said I adored you,
And you tripped in your reply.

When I asked about your day,
And you didn't hear mine.

When I saw you again,
And you didn't smile.

I don't know what I feel.
Anger for your false words,
Sadness, or emptiness,
Depression, heart in discord,
Blaming myself all the while.

Before realising it was you
Or rather them
Or your wretched fixation
With those other dancers.

All you need to know,
Is that I really cared,
You were my euphony.
I just wish that you'd
Took time to listen.

BEAUTY FROM BLACKNESS

Sometimes I see the world as my canvas,
With a strike of the brush, I give birth
To such sickeningly sweet sunsets,
Smearing a happy ending for myself.
I don't know how I will get there,
But I don't really care,
The idea is still there.

Of course, there must be sacrifices,
My brush must become a sword,
A sword of my own salvation
And my terrible indulgence.
My hollow eyes give a piercing blow,
Before everything disappears
In a blur of blackness.

After the dripping settles, all that is left
Is Nature, in all her glory,
But in all of her imperfections, too.
Those make the work interesting.
They say that's where true beauty lies,
But the real beauty is in the absence
Of intrusive feet.

CRYSTAL EYES

I looked into your eyes
And I realised
Those weren't your real eyes,
They had crystallised
And become crystal eyes,
All because you had senselessly idolised,
Staring endlessly into your idol's eyes.

Trapped in a dream, you were fantasising
Of something that could never come to fruition.
I don't know why you found that surprising,
But you always did lack basic intuition.

What were you expecting from a face of stone?
To grant you absolution, the gift of freedom?
That is a quest you must embark on alone,
Without the aid of your imaginary kingdom.

Sitting on your hands, you waited and waited,
For some sign or light, disembodied voices,
To release you from the misery you created,
The pain manifested from you, your choices.

But still you waited for your precious instructor
To tell you where to go next, how best to proceed.
A deceptive disguise he may wear, the dictator,
But will gladly let you suffer and let you bleed.

It is not too late; you can still set yourself free,
Detach your mind from meaningless words,
And shatter the cursed glass, so you can see
The true, naked world, and strive onwards.

THE SILENT FORCE

Why is that, when we talk,
We don't say anything at all?

Something that troubles us, consumes us
Is not spoken.
A lingering, crushing doubt
Is simply ignored.

But what is preventing me
From firing my feelings into the air,
From throwing my thoughts to your ears,
What is this unknown, impenetrable force?

I'm not certain it's even there at all,
It might all be in my head,
Existing solely in my own imagination.
Or is that what you want me to think?

But maybe it is the fear of what will happen,
If I attempt to break that barrier,
Will our shaky foundation
Crumble into dust once and for all?

Perhaps I'll just play the waiting game,
And hope that silence will soften the blow.

DREAM'S END

Waking from a whirlpool of confusion
All suddenly became clear,
Eyes no longer stained from illusion,
Nothing left to fear.

A curious journey it had been,
Everyone in strange roles,
Unprepared for wonders seen,
Doomed to be lost souls.

Their avatars were yet retrieved,
Moulded in different form,
The former strife starting to recede,
Lost in that dark storm.

We battled on till we pierced its eye,
Spilling out to the other side,
Fate constricted us to this, or to die,
Swallowed by the dark tide.

Our other selves were lost that day,
The water born us anew,
Each hazy regret now washed away,
The light saw us through.

We saw it over the miasma of mist,
The lighthouse of hope.
We were chosen, marked on the list,
To cross over the tightrope.

REVOLUTION'S DUST

The city was cold that night,
Snow covered the scars and pain
It had endured in its plight,
But the white washes away in rain.

It could not freeze the suffering
Or pull the streets back in time,
No longer did the insurgents sing
Their revolutionary rhyme.

Dusty roads flooded with silence,
The city's spirit bound, choked,
They sang not words of violence,
But ruler's wrath was still provoked.

A lone figure emerges in cold mist,
A warrior once, now nobody,
One who said no, dared to resist,
Now a shell stripped of its tenacity.

He smirks at such a sorry state,
Stepping over fallen comrades,
Taken by the fierce goddess Fate,
The stench of sorrow pervades.

Here where forgotten heroes bled
He wanders without remorse,
For them no tears will be shed,
Nor for their foolhardy cause.

The road ahead splits into two,
One path to mindless compliance,
Or a mortality to escape through,
That ultimate sacrifice and defiance.

And so, his path is the latter,
Bravery still burning, a noble choice,
But an action that shall not matter
In a world usurped of its voice.

THE LAST TRAIN

The train judders to a halt,
Doors flying open like wings,
The final destination reached,
Terminus is in plain sight.

A station unmanned, no keeper.
No windows, only steel shutters,
The signs are faded, rusting,
The name no longer matters.

The air is so still, so lifeless,
Not even a whiff of wind.
There are no songs in this town,
And no stories to tell.

Dead flowers wilt in brown grass,
Shop fronts boarded up, forgotten.
Far gone echoes of the glory days,
The heady times that can't return.

Crumbling steps lead to nowhere,
Rusting girders support nothing,
A landing stage with no arrivals,
And no attractions to allure.

And yet this dismal destination
Is still on this train's itinerary,
An eternal dot on the map
Where feet no longer tread.

SEED OF DOUBT

You always have something to say,
Drowning out the drunken revelry,
Doubts that drip with derision,
Splashed with scorn and disdain.
You snicker at me, cold and mocking,
I surrender to it, and swallow it all.

Scuttling back to the dingy corner,
I approach no one, alone in the dark.
My refuge from rejection, a safe place,
Or so you keep on telling me.
You'll never be like them, you say,
So I stay hidden, ruler of the rejects.

I sip at my current elixir of choice,
Losing count as my senses elude me.
Would another finally drown you out?
Or at least put an end to my misery.
But alas, you still prattle on and on,
Slicing through esteem like it's wet paper.

Oh, stop looking at her, pitiful worm,
She wouldn't bother looking twice,
She'd laugh in your pasty little face,
As would her snivelling male cohorts
Who just want to slither into her skirt,
But they'd have more chance than you.

Look at yourself, useless cretin!
As if a mumbling misfit like you
Could hope to forge anything at all
With the normals all around you.
You'd only fuck it up somehow,
So stop and spare us the wailing.

Stop saying that!! I know I know!
Your voice is the harshest poison,
Torturing me endlessly, mercilessly.
If this burden is the price for breathing,
I will drink till I see only blackness,
And be alone with the sweet silence.

UNQUENCHABLE

He stands alone,
Unbound and unchained
From this tiresome terrain.
The untouchable man.

Unadorned he roams,
His flesh impervious
To heat and flame,
And piddling pebbles.

Unfazed and always focused,
Standing in the chaos,
The centre of destruction,
Yet the harbinger of creation.

Unmoved by the known world,
He seeks a new summit,
Where smoke screams skyward,
Engulfing the ennui below.

Unafraid, with no regret,
His fists hammer down,
Breaking the path forth
To unleash new beginnings.

Unabashed, he stands calm,
In the whirlwind of fire,
An unholy circle dancing
Around an aura of arrogance.

Unravaged by this inferno,
The notion of pain
Does not enter or intrude
Upon his brazen brain.

Uncertain of the world's course,
But ready for judgement's rain,
Channelling the cylinder of magma
He fires the future into the sky.

THE STARDUST SHADOW

In the darkness of his pit, he stirs,
That man skulking in the shadows,
That man with the intricate system,
The man with the obsession.
Before it all fell apart
And devoured the man he once was.

That man stares into his smeared glass,
As memories of misjudgement endure.
Relics of regret litter his disordered desk,
Cards from foolhardy, misguided games,
The dice with their accusing snake eyes
That taunt him relentlessly, evermore.

That man had dreams once, ambitions
To conquer each and every house of cards.
All remains now are tarnished beermats,
And matchbooks cataloguing each downfall,
That world now merely a malty puddle,
The once bright lights now but a memory.

That man had other urges inside him too,
An animalistic addiction for the siren's touch.
Craving release of their twisted stimulation,
He succumbed, soon seduced by them all,
But now he is alone, a ghost in the form of
The penniless fool, his soul empty too.

That man now hides, head in desert sand,
Ignoring the detritus of debt and demands.
He drowns in a misery of his own making,
Hoping to elude those heartless hounds
That still harangue him for half his worth,
Pursuing till the ends of the earth.

In the darkness of his pit, he sinks,
That man fading into the shadows,
That man with the intricate system,
That man with the obsession.
Before it all fell apart,
And drained him of his very being.

THE SECRET LIBRARY

Down the winding stairs
A whole other world lies.
A labyrinth of literature,
A torrent of tomes,
Streaming their secret words
From its sprawling shelves.

Sparkling dust clouds the air,
A musty yet welcome aroma,
The scent of slowly unfurling
That first beckoning page,
Opening the papery portal
To boundless, infinite wonder.

Few tread this uncharted forest,
But all find their own path
In the form of covert words
Guiding them in their plight.
They speak it with no sound,
But answer every question.

These mutters hang ghostily
In the stifling, eerie stillness,
Reincarnated as rows of relics
In the unending passages
That dreamers are doomed
To get hopelessly lost in.

This escape is set in stone
Or scribed in eternal ink.
This place is their haven,
Their own hallowed halls
Of heroes and heretics alike
Who speak to their hearts.

Reality still remains outside,
It is the literary life force
That scribblers thrive upon,
And there it will always be,
Beyond that creaky door,
Tethering us to the tangible.

THE CONTROLLER

It watched from misted glass,
The explanation of all action,
Of all events that occurred,
The fierce eyes of the Controller.

Marvelling at its onerous work,
It assigned tasks for loyal denizens,
Who obeyed with no objection,
Shuffling by in enforced direction.

The city that its hand had created
Was forever expanding, evolving,
New structures were materialising
In the metropolis of his mind.

It knew no barriers nor limits,
A place bursting with possibility,
Changes at a tap of its digits,
Alas, it gives but also takes away.

Forsaken followers soon vanished,
Consigned to a dark repression,
Locked behind sealed doors,
Deep within its enduring mind.

Such is the price of this onus,
Not all fruits bore would survive,
Some would wither in obscurity,
Denied the chance to thrive.

Others would still remain,
But confined to tedium,
Chained to tiresome chores,
All irrelevant to the true cause.

The same paths always trod,
Some leading nowhere at all,
Others loops with no logic,
A more fearsome fate, perhaps.

Perhaps this was inevitable,
Indeed the throttling towers
Now dwarfed their populace,
Infinite space just an illusion.

Yet the Controller was powerless,
There were forces higher still
Who denied further frontiers,
Thus the dream collapsed within.

A single, lonely tear dropped
From its almighty, all-seeing eye,
Grieving the fate once again
Of its most coveted creations.

Yet this pain must be bore
For the greater good of all,
Circularity is the curse of this,
Cleansing, its kindness to them.

The consumption is not cruel,
It is mercy masked as progress,
Sparing them from the truth
Of a world that will still go on.
It watched from shattered glass,

The explanation of all action,
Of all events that occurred,
The weary eyes of the Controller.

STOLEN HEARTS

I steal the hearts of mousy men,
Their pure, pulsing hearts,
Infused with incessant spirit
And ripe for dismembering.

It is not a simple snatch,
Rather a prolonged extraction,
A cold, cunning plan
Of measured manipulation.

All of course, are unaware,
My plan cleverly veiled
In the guise of caring bonds,
A deceptive partnership.

Promises will pour freely
From my mendacious mouth,
But none shall be kept,
Broken as they are spoken.

Lies languish like dead flowers,
As I release the weeds of deceit,
Their vines trapping my victim,
Perceptions callously twisted.

Their pain is a dreamy drug,
The vice that can't be kicked,
I tremble to naivety's tears,
Quivering at pathetic questions.

I listen just long enough,
But then I pounce and snatch,
Bringing that final blow,
Clawing till they squeal.

Their pleas are pitiful,
Yet painfully musical,
The same old song,
But one I shall never tire of.

They shriek and squirm,
As I wrench them out,
Their precious vital organ
That trusts far too much.

I steal the hearts of mousy men,
Their pure, pulsing hearts,
Drained of futile desires,
Now tainted by the truth.

GUARDIAN OF GOLD

The sunset leaves its golden trail,
A shining bridge to the arid land,
Bestowing its light on bleary eyes,
Showing the promised mountains.
It sets speedily into their summits,
The sky swirling into sickly patterns,
Like the countless cocktails
That the crowds have consumed.

That glorious golden eye peeks
From behind the misty hills.
Alas, weary it grows of the watch,
Now it must darken to slumber,
Shedding its shimmering armour
So it may withstand another day
As golden guardian and awakener
Of the inebriated masses.

SHALLOW AS TIME

It's always slipping away from us,
That slithery beast called Time.
Speech just vanishes into thin air,
Slivers that splinter into fragments,
Worn by Time like tarnished silver.

Deep thoughts cannot hope to surface
In rooms corrupted by intrusive noise,
Precious quiet just out of reach.
The senseless ones spout so much,
But in reality, reveal so very little.

Time still drips away into life's basin,
Slowly, but with stubborn intent.
But it will not be Time that takes us,
Rather the uproar of the Unenlightened,
And their speeches that smother us.

If only they'd stop, for a mere second,
To listen to the sweet song of Eternity.
So wondrous it is, simply in its absence
Of any sound at all, not one note,
But still unveiling from its secret shroud.

As once stated by one wise with words,
Written into forever, not merely said,
The harmonies that are hushed
Are often more pleasant a taste,
Than the ones heard every day.

This battle is one raging continually
Between the depth of the inner voice,
And the outward that overpowers it.
Yet we must fight above the clamour,
And regain the golden city of forever.

THE ETERNAL DEEP

The mountains fade soundlessly into fog,
But palaces loudly proclaim themselves.
The sea yawns from their stone walls,
Where underneath so many wonders lie,
Their beauty not displayed so wantonly,
As only certain eyes may gaze upon them.

Far you must venture for such visions,
But exhaustion will soon evaporate,
Dissolving into a rush of exhilaration,
No words that come seem worthy.
These sights are fixed and nameless,
To denote them degrades their mystery.

The world above carries on regardless,
The desert's denizens dawdling onward,
Past those gates of supposed paradise.
Humdrum hangs in the air, a weight
That sends them sinking, not into the sea
But hopelessly, helplessly into themselves.

THE SIMPLE JOY

There used to be so much surprise,
Waiting beyond those stairs.
Boxes of all shapes and sizes,
Teasing us until tomorrow
When they would be torn, exposed,
Innards taken by tiny, tremulous hands.

Hidden within is what we hungered for,
What we harried and hassled for,
Until the overlords finally relented
And granted us our gaudy trinkets,
But under agreement of sealing them
Until some absurdly arbitrary date.

Yet the greatest gifts of all
Were the ones we could not predict.
Unexpected booty soon uncovered,
To keep impish rogues on their toes,
The wait suddenly becoming worth
Restraining our rascally ways for.

Like unwrapping the usual candies,
So unassuming they'd look, ordinary,
Until finding that sweet centre,
A secret flavour discovered,
Heaven to our innocent tongues,
Delirium in a tiny package.

Yes, a simple pleasure indeed,
Playing until pitch-black night,
With no cares or concerns,
And no place to be in the morn.
Precious gifts given to us by magic,
With no exchange expected.

But now, once we have grown,
It slips through our wrinkly fingers,
The simple joy of surprise.
We are asked what we desire,
Instead of anyone guessing,
So we long for those simple days.

The simple, precious days
Where anything surprised our little minds.

THE RAIN OF REDEMPTION

You whispered to me in the rain,
Sharing the secrets of your soul,
Stories that no other has heard.
You'd been waiting to tell them,
But you needed to know for sure
That the words would not be wasted,
That every one would be duly listened to
By the non-judgemental knight.

The world hammers down around us,
But always my armour will withstand
And until now, guard me from it.
But for you, and only ever you,
I shall lower my suspecting shield
And show the self I tightly concealed
Deep within my cautious mind,
A heavy burden I can lift at last.

We spill not our blood, only secrets
Beneath the storm surrounding us.
Though the steel rain always falls,
It cannot break through our bond.
For it is built stronger than any metal,
And once the storm has settled,
We shall still be standing,
Sealed in our own serenity.

THE VICIOUS VEIL

She smirks as she sits with them,
Sipping from her snifter like a snake,
She listens, but doesn't comfort.
Rather, stows the sob stories away,
Amassing bullets to bite back with
Should they ever dare to slur her.

The false smiles, the forced laughter
All emit from her caustically coral lips.
She rolls her eyes at their ramblings,
Scoffs at their pissy little problems,
Stringing along her fair-weather chums
Until stinging them steadily one by one.

They all trust far too easily,
Blissfully ignorant of her trickery
And her cunningly cruel game,
Where they are simply the pieces
On a board so deadly treacherous,
Into her trap they will surely fall.

Each move pulses with a purpose,
Every word is carefully chosen.
The meticulous mask never slips,
The face of malice never revealed.
The raven's claws ever concealed
In the gaudiness of glittery pink nails.

It's a vicious veil indeed that she wears,
Woven from the woe of pitiable worms,
One that deceives all who perceive it
That a heart lies within her wiry frame.
A grand and marvellous delusion indeed,
Perfected by a pitiless wench of stone.

AN ODE TO ORANGE

O Orange, that shade in-between!
Born from red and yellow's coition,
Blue bonds with latter to make green,
Or purple if the former is its fusion,
So promiscuous, those primary ensigns!
But such a child of colour they created,
A fiery complement to its blue cousin,
Radicals realised this as they painted.

O Orange, first without designation,
A portmanteau of your parentage,
Before found in bounty of plantation,
A sweet fruit, its hue the same visage.
Light and plant's dance is a tinting trail
To leaf and crop alike, sharing your shade,
Blanketing the trees in their autumnal veil
When the air chills, and verdancy fades.

O Orange, the flame of fertility!
Bringing life to human and harvest,
Birthed from mothers of mortality,
As well as those at their behest.
Fiery flowing dress in alluring frame,
Or lighting the Lady's locks lavishly,
Madness sheened in a glowing mane,
Still admirers fawn for her slavishly.

O Orange, our radiant guide!
A beacon in both sky and sea,
A badge rescuers wear with pride,

But also the dress of depravity.
Tortured souls locked away, sealed
In a fortress enclosed in fog,
Only beaming bridge is revealed
In misty bay within grey smog.

O Orange, great opposing force!
To the subdued calmness of blue,
Yet still its companion, of course,
On duality they depend, as two.
Whatever faiths conflict and endure,
They share the same great space,
And brave that same stormy shore,
Casting waves of change to all places.

O Orange, the ray of reinvention!
Adorned upon enlightened souls
Who pick the key of transformation,
Committed to their solitary roles.
They teach the truth, and illuminate
The path to the great, single spirit,
Reality but an obstacle to renunciate
In the quest to unmask and hear it.

O Orange, mark of the primal!
Of tigers who lurk at night,
Whose shape is so frightful,
A bright beast darkly striped.
A more cunning creature lurks too,
Slender and sneakier, skills it needs
To evade pursuers forcing through,
Whose fire threatens both breeds.

O Orange, that clownish colour!
The warming glow that energises
Those whose zest has turned sour,
Now seekers of sweet surprises.
They dance with danger brazenly,
Unashamed of their true being,
They present themselves playfully,
Never knowing a light so freeing.

O Orange, shade of setting sky!
As one day ends, you paint the air,
The sign that darkness is nigh,
Whereupon you light your flare
In lamps and lanterns along a lane
And in the twinkles so high above.
Our protector in uncertain terrain,
A familiar flicker in the eyes we love.

O Orange, the unappreciated!
The choice of the unconventional,
But I compose this ode inebriated
By your sweet shades, so sensual
And magical to my enchanted eyes,
So that I can show others your beauty,
As artists did with their delicate dyes,
So that they may see your true majesty.

TIDE OF TIME

Once you could do no wrong,
Do no harm, bring no hurt,
But time has tainted you.
A nebulous image, fading,
But the stains still remain,
The sad smudges and smears
From those vain, heady hopes
Of what we could have been.

Number one, a few good days,
Some snatches of sentiment,
But most thoughts were taken
By another, more proven pair
Of whom you were preoccupied.
Thus the trickles of time alone
Could not hope to weigh against
That settled state you all shared.

Then came you, number two,
The promise of far too much
In rapid heat of melting moments.
But all part of your grander plan,
To possess not only my penance,
But my very perception of things.
Twisting and turning them all,
Until reality finally resisted me.

It came back before you, Three.
My, you were a fickle one indeed,
First foretelling a thorough future
But then closing our book abruptly.
You then opened it once again,
Yet then say I misinterpret its words,
And fire unpleasant ones back at me,
I say nothing back, tiring of our tale.

And finally there was you, Four.
You and me kindred in many things,
The words pouring more easily,
My ramblings taken seriously.
But fear grabbed hold, freezing you,
Meaning we could go no further,
Your brain's barrier blocking us
And breaking me to surrender.

I promised to do no more,
To not bear pointless pain.
But time soon taught me
That hope must hurt
And desire must damage
For us to sense its purpose
And exultant tears to emerge
When the right you is found.

THE GENTLE DRAGON

You wrap me in your wings
And I will always hold on
Until what dawn's light brings
And awake with you, my gentle dragon.

You have that fire in your heart,
Which you breathe in passionate blaze,
Yet tenderness is also a part
I see of you, when holding your gaze.

You carry me through dark of night,
Sharing secrets of the moon,
But staying with me until the light
Breaks through, to share morning soon.

You keep me up in the sky
Whenever life makes me fall.
To brighter days I will surely fly
With my precious one, my all.

You are a warm-hearted beast,
Your spikes and marks all telling a tale,
Those being but the very least
Of your beauty, to me you unveil.

You wrap me in your wings
Forever I will hold on
For what future skies bring
And journey with you, my gentle dragon.

THE SURFACING

As light lacerates the haze,
My statue rebuilds itself.
A landmark in this deep maze
That guided me back to myself.

Inside is a mind now focused,
As unclouded as a mirror.
For a mind kept polished,
The path to serenity is clear.

Mind and body meld into one,
The disparity can now dissolve,
And no harsh words can stun
The power of this new resolve.

I channel this from great depth,
Finally finding my elusory centre,
Tapped from where I draw breath,
Fear and doubt shall not enter.

Within, all is composed and calm
And tempted not by distraction.
So I need not bear any harm,
If charged by this concentration.

But as I live on, still I must learn,
New lessons I shall forever find,
And to some I must return
To keep open my thriving mind.

Soon it shall be enlightened
To the true nature of things
And no longer so frightened
Of what tomorrow may bring.

As light lacerates the haze,
My statue stands tall.
A landmark in this deep maze
That can withstand it all.

ABOUT THE AUTHOR

Stuart Peacock is an avid reader of literature who has been writing himself in some form or another since he was six-years-old. He was raised in Clacton-on-Sea and went on to receive a BA in English Literature at the University of Essex. He now works supporting individuals with autism, still writing in his spare time, and lives with his partner, Russell, in Colchester, Essex.
His favourite fiction author is Margaret Atwood, and favourite poets include Charles Baudelaire, John Keats, Percy Bysshe Shelley, and William Blake.

www.apexpublishing.co.uk

www.ingramcontent.com/pod-product-compliance
Lightning Source LLC
Chambersburg PA
CBHW031432040426
42444CB00006B/774